How does an EARTHQUAKE become a TSUNAMI?

Linda Tagliaferro

Raintree

Chicago, Illinois

www.heinemannraintree.com
Visit our website to find out more information about Heinemann-Raintree books.

To order:
☎ Phone 888-454-2279
💻 Visit www.heinemannraintree.com to browse our catalog and order online.

Edited by David Andrews and Laura Knowles
Designed by Richard Parker and Wagtail
Original illustrations © Capstone Global Library, LLC 2010
Illustrated by Jeff Edwards
Picture research by Hannah Taylor and Sally Claxton
Originated by Modern Age Repro House Ltd
Printed and bound in China by CTPS

14 13 12 11 10
10 9 8 7 6 5 4 3 2

Library of Congress Cataloging-in-Publication Data
Tagliaferro, Linda.
  How does an earthquake become a tsunami? / Linda Tagliaferro.
     p. cm. -- (How does it happen?)
  Includes bibliographical references and index.
  ISBN 978-1-4109-3446-8 (hc) -- ISBN 978-1-4109-3454-3 (pb)
  1. Tsunami--Juvenile literature. 2. Waves--Juvenile literature. 3. Earthquakes--Juvenile literature. 4. Plate tectonics--Juvenile literature. I. Title.
  GC221.5.T34 2008
  551.46'37--dc22
                    2008052643

Acknowledgments

The author and publishers are grateful to the following for permission to reproduce copyright material: Corbis pp. **4** (Jeremy Horner), **5** (Bettmann), **6, 9** (Roger Ressmeyer), **11** (Grant Smith), **13** (Lloyd Cluff), **18** (Bettmann), **19** (Wolfgang Kaehler), **23** (Supri/Reuters), **26** (EPA/Nani Afrida); istockphoto **background image** (© Dean Turner); PA Photos pp. **21** (AP Photo/ Gemunu Amarasinghe), **22** (AP Photo/ Eugene Hoshiko), **24** (AP Photo/Eranga Jayawardena), **25** (AP Photo/ Gemunu Amarasinghe), **27** (Edmond Terakopian), **29** (AP Photo/Fadlan Arman Syam); Rex Features p. **17** (Sipa Press).

Cover photograph of earthquake damage in Sichuan province, Central China (top) reproduced with permission of Rex Features/Sipa Press and a pipeline wave (bottom) reproduced with permission of Shuterstock/©Mana Photo.

Every effort has been made to contact copyright holders of any material reproduced in this book. Any omissions will be rectified in subsequent printings if notice is given to the publisher.

All the Internet addresses (URLs) given in this book were valid at the time of going to press. However, due to the dynamic nature of the Internet, some addresses may have changed, or sites may have changed or ceased to exist since publication. While the author and Publishers regret any inconvenience this may cause readers, no responsibility for any such changes can be accepted by either the author or the Publishers.

Contents

Some words are shown in bold, **like this**. You can find out what they mean by looking in the glossary.

Wall of Water!

A **tsunami** is a giant wave. Tsunamis can seem strange and unpredictable. One moment waves are crashing against the beach as usual. Water rolls in and out at an even pace. Then, without warning, the water suddenly disappears. It is as if something has swallowed the ocean.

A huge wave crashes onto the beach in Thailand in 2004.

Minutes later, that disappearing **tide** rushes forward. Now it is a massive wall of water. It pushes past the beach and over barriers, roads, and even homes. People run screaming to escape the destruction.

A tsunami destroyed these houses in Hilo, Hawaii in 1960.

The tsunami may have seemed to come out of nowhere, but it could have been predicted. Hours before, an **earthquake** shook the ocean floor. The movement of the ocean floor pushed aside a mass of water. This caused waves to form and grow larger and larger, creating a deadly tsunami.

A Greek thinker

In 426 BCE the Greek historian Thucydides (say "Thoo-SID-id-eez") described how the water along the shore disappeared and then returned in a huge wave to flood a town. He noted that earthquakes had also been happening in the area. Thucydides became one of the first people to suggest a connection between earthquakes and tsunamis.

Layers of Earth

The story of **earthquakes** and **tsunamis** starts deep inside Earth. The ground we are standing on is just a small part of Earth. Like the skin of an onion, the hard **crust** we live on is just the top of many layers that make up our planet.

The surface of Earth is called the crust.

Earth as seen from space

The **mantle** sits below the crust. It is made up of hot, semi-solid rock. In the center of Earth is the **core**. This is made up of two parts. The hot, liquid outer core surrounds the inner core, which is mostly solid iron and nickel.

Earth has many layers. The crust we stand on is just a small part of the whole planet.

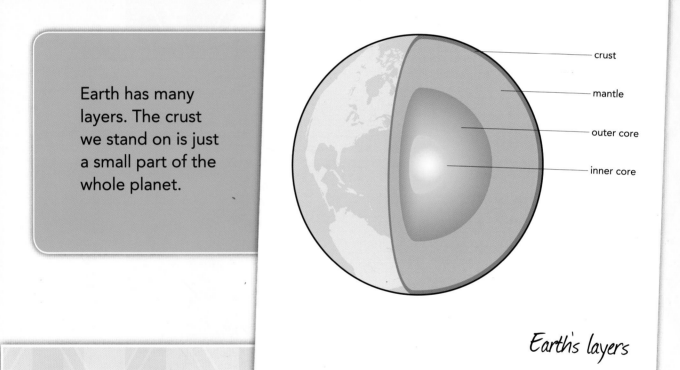

crust

mantle

outer core

inner core

Earth's layers

How deep?

How far down are the different layers of Earth? The crust is about 40 kilometers (25 miles) thick on average—but it is thinner under the ocean than on land. The mantle is about 2,900 kilometers (1,800 miles) thick. The core is about 3,450 kilometers (2,100 miles) thick.

Is Earth's Crust Moving?

We live on Earth's top layer, the **crust**. The ground we are standing on seems very sturdy. It does not seem to be moving at all. But scientists say this upper part of Earth, the crust, is broken up into many parts. These huge parts fit together like a jigsaw puzzle. These giant puzzle pieces are called **tectonic plates**.

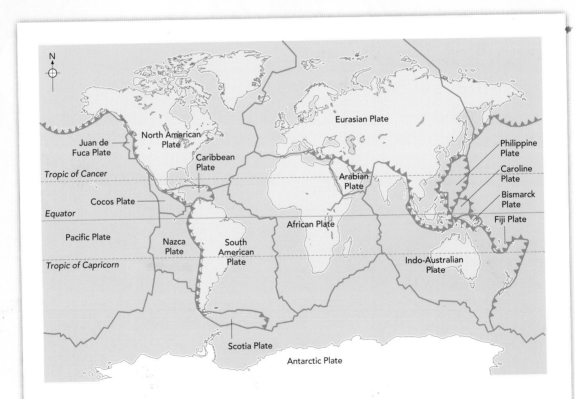

Earth's tectonic plates

This map shows how Earth's tectonic plates fit together. The red triangles show where one plate is sliding under another plate.

Moving parts

These plates sometimes move toward one another and start to push together. Sometimes the plates move in opposite directions, away from one another. The plates move slowly, so we usually do not feel the motion. But there are times when we do feel the movements. This is when **earthquakes** shake the ground beneath us.

Above and below

Tectonic plates that lie under the ocean are called **oceanic plates**. Tectonic plates that lie under the continents are called **continental plates**. Some tectonic plates are bigger than an entire continent.

This break in Earth's crust is in California's Sierra Nevada mountain range.

What Causes Earthquakes?

An **earthquake** is a sudden, often violent shaking of the ground. What makes this happen? It begins when two of Earth's **tectonic plates** meet. They push up against one another, which creates a lot of tension.

The **crust** is very strong and can withstand a lot of pressure. But after many years of pushing against one another, the plates cannot withstand the strain. Suddenly, they shift past one another.

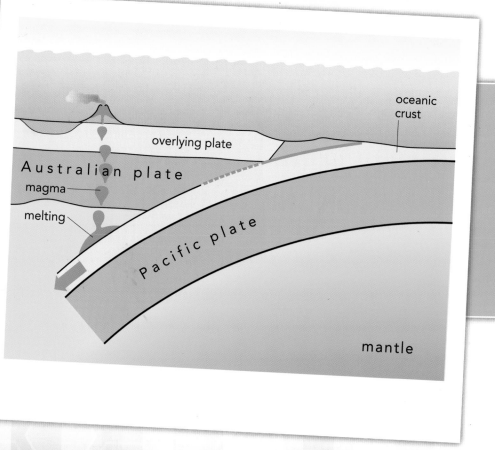

This drawing shows how the Pacific plate is sliding underneath the Australian plate.

All this slipping and sliding of land sends out **shock waves** in all directions. These waves cause the ground to shake. Sometimes, when plates collide, one huge tectonic plate slides underneath another one. This can cause very big earthquakes. After an earthquake, there are usually **aftershocks**, or smaller earthquakes.

In 1989, an earthquake in San Francisco, California severely damaged this apartment house and many other buildings.

The Richter scale

Scientists measure the size of earthquakes with a number on the **Richter scale**. The higher the number, the more destructive an earthquake can be. We usually cannot feel earthquakes that are below 2.0. Earthquakes that measure 6.0 on the Richter scale are strong. Very dangerous earthquakes are 8.0 or higher.

Earthquake Zones

Many of the world's **earthquakes** occur in the **Ring of Fire**, a vast area surrounding the Pacific Ocean. The edges of some of Earth's **tectonic plates** meet in this area.

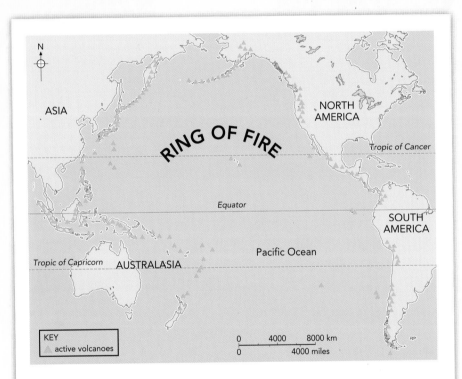

The Ring of Fire stretches far around the Pacific Ocean

Since the plates meet up there, they can bump into one another. They can also move away from or slide past one another. This movement can cause earthquakes and volcanic eruptions.

Earthquakes are common in other areas, too. Beyond the Ring of Fire, earthquakes are common in the Alpide belt, which includes some mountains in Europe and Asia. Many underwater earthquakes also occur in the mid-Atlantic ridge, an area on the Atlantic Ocean floor. There, molten (hot, melted) **magma** from Earth's **mantle** rises up through huge cracks in Earth's **crust**.

Whose fault?

Faults are big fractures in Earth's crust. Many faults are found on the edges of Earth's tectonic plates. Most earthquakes happen there. One large fault zone in California, called the San Andreas Fault Zone, only moves about 5 centimeters (2 inches) each year. This is only about the same rate that people's fingernails grow. But strong earthquakes have occurred there.

The San Andreas fault

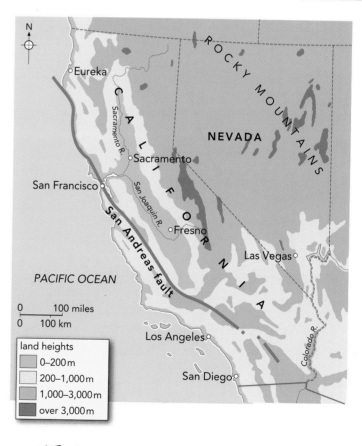

The fault is about 1,300 kilometers long

Speeding to Shore

During an **earthquake**, rocks along a **fault** at the **tectonic plate** boundary break apart and slide against each other. Rocks on one side of the fault rapidly go down and the other side goes up. The rapid movement of the fault blocks at the bottom of the ocean pushes the water above.

Ocean water gets pushed up when tectonic plates collide.

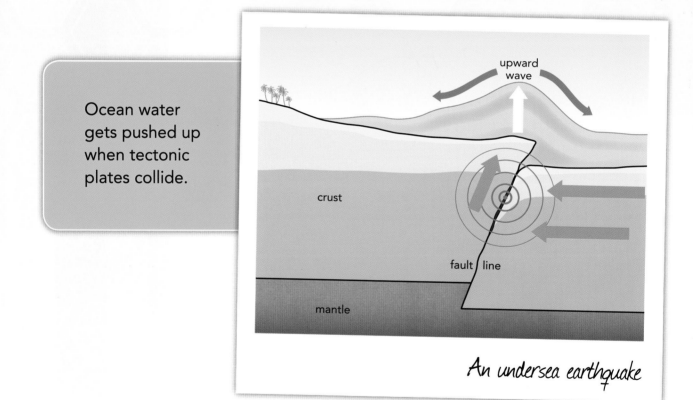

upward wave

crust

fault line

mantle

An undersea earthquake

The moving water creates a ripple, like a pebble thrown in a pond. These ripples begin as wide, shallow waves. They can be as far apart as 100 kilometers (60 miles). They are so gradual that people in an ocean liner would not notice sailing over them.

As the waves move in the direction of the shore, however, they become shorter, higher, and faster. They begin to travel as fast as a jet plane.

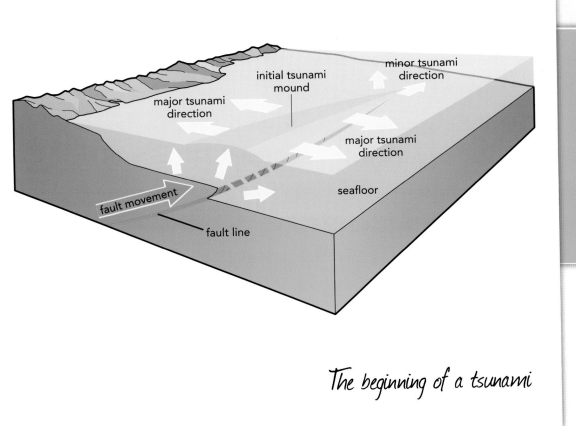

The beginning of a tsunami

This diagram shows how a tsunami spreads outward from the fault line where it began.

Tidal wave or tsunami?
Although some people call these huge waves **tidal waves**, the correct word is *tsunamis*. Tidal waves are unusually large waves created by wind and the **tides** (the natural rising and falling of the ocean).

Danger on the Beach!

As waves caused by underwater **earthquakes** get closer to the shore, they bump into land. The bottom of the ocean is very deep, but the land surrounding beaches is not.

When a speeding wave meets the shallow land, the bottom of the wave slows down. But the rest of the wave keeps going fast. With nowhere to go but up, the water piles up into a gigantic wave.

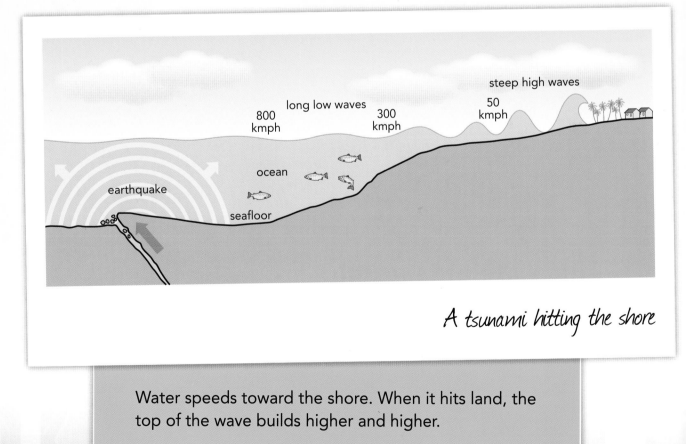

steep high waves

long low waves

800 kmph

300 kmph

50 kmph

ocean

earthquake

seafloor

A tsunami hitting the shore

Water speeds toward the shore. When it hits land, the top of the wave builds higher and higher.

Sometimes the ocean recedes, or pulls back from the shore, as the coming wave draws in more water. The beach will seem bigger just minutes before the **tsunami** comes crashing down.

This photo shows the ocean pulling back from the shore before a tsunami strikes.

Continuing waves

The first tsunami wave is followed by many more. There can be great distances between waves. The first may not be the tallest or the most dangerous. These waves can continue for hours.

Landslide!

Tsunamis are not always caused by **earthquakes**. They can also be the result of giant landslides or volcanic eruptions on land or underwater. In May 1883 huge clouds of black smoke soared to the sky in Indonesia (see map on page 20). They came from a **volcano** on the island of Krakatoa, between the islands of Java and Sumatra.

This drawing shows the volcano on Krakatoa during its eruption. The land around it has been flooded by the ocean.

Krakatoa, 1883

Then in August of that year, the volcano erupted violently. A powerful series of blasts almost blew apart the entire island. Hot ashes and burning rocks from the volcano traveled at high speeds, killing people in Indonesian villages across the water.

Almost two-thirds of Krakatoa, and parts of nearby islands, collapsed into the water. This huge landslide produced tsunamis 40 meters (130 feet) high. These tsunamis sped to nearby shores, destroying entire villages. Most of the 36,000 people who died from Krakatoa's volcanic eruption were killed by the sudden tsunamis.

Krakatoa today

Today Krakatoa Island is much smaller than it was before the violent eruption.

A deafening noise

The sounds of Krakatoa's explosion were so loud that people as far away as 4,800 kilometers (3,000 miles) could hear the noise!

2004 Tsunami

On December 26, 2004, a huge undersea **earthquake**, measuring 9.0 on the **Richter scale**, rocked the ocean floor of the Indian Ocean in Asia.

An undersea earthquake off the coast of Indonesia caused tsunamis near and far.

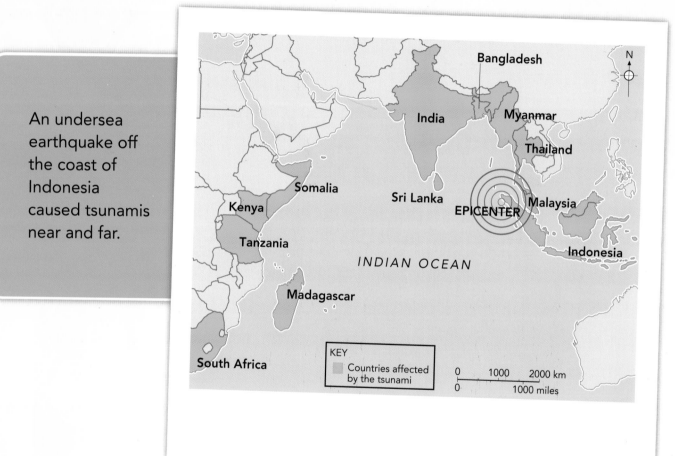

Bangladesh

India

Myanmar

Thailand

Somalia

Sri Lanka

Kenya

EPICENTER

Malaysia

Tanzania

Indonesia

INDIAN OCEAN

Madagascar

South Africa

KEY

Countries affected by the tsunami

0   1000   2000 km
0   1000 miles

N

The pressure had been building up for more than 100 years in this part of Earth's **crust**. Finally, the lower **tectonic plate** was pushed underneath the upper plate, which carries most of Southeast Asia.

The earthquake rumbled off the coast of the island nation of Indonesia. The violent shaking lasted for eight minutes. Billions of tons of water were forced upward by the movements of the plates.

The immense earthquake created **tsunamis** that killed over 200,000 people in 11 countries. Some of the waves were as high as 10 meters (33 feet), taller than a three-story building.

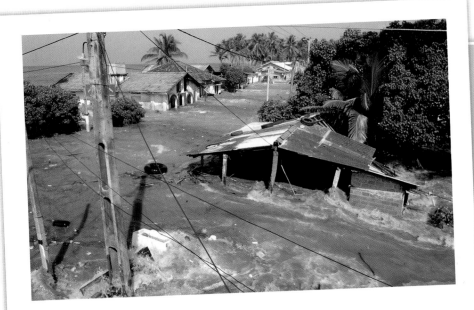

Entire villages in Indonesia were destroyed by a tsunami.

A powerful force

The force of the Indian Ocean earthquake in December 2004 was so great that it not only affected nearby areas. It also triggered small earthquakes as far away as Alaska.

A Disaster with No Warning

In Sumatra, Indonesia, no one knew that danger was fast approaching. A half-hour after the undersea **earthquake** rocked the ocean floor, a huge **tsunami** sped to nearby Sumatra. The powerful wave pounded the coastline, killing tens of thousands of people. It destroyed entire villages.

Many buildings were destroyed when a tsunami crashed into this village in Sri Lanka, Asia.

But the tsunamis did not stop there. More of the immense waves raced to Thailand. There, the waves carried off tourists who had been relaxing on the beach.

Tsunamis also crashed down on the coasts of Sri Lanka and India. These devastating waves hit other areas, including the faraway African countries of Somalia and Kenya.

The force of a tsunami pushed this boat inland into an Indonesian village. It landed on a house.

To the ends of the Earth

The strongest tsunamis on December 26, 2004, reached countries in Asia and Africa. But as the waves sent out by the earthquake got weaker, they traveled very far and reached the Arctic and Antarctic.

Danger After the Tsunami

Even after the giant waves finish their path of destruction, there are still great dangers. Survivors who have been injured need immediate medical care, or they could get sick or even die.

Many survivors are left without homes. They need food and water, but they have no place to get them and no place to cook meals. Some children have been separated from their parents.

"Baby 81" survived the tsunami and was brought back to his parents.

Baby 81

In Sri Lanka a baby boy was swept out of his mother's arms by the 2004 tsunami. Luckily, the baby was found alive, but all alone in a pile of garbage. He was brought to a hospital, where he was known as "Baby 81" because he was the 81st patient brought there. Months later, he was reunited with his family.

The floods may carry **bacteria** (tiny living things) and spread disease. Mosquitoes can breed in waters that are stagnant (not flowing). They can spread dangerous diseases like **malaria**.

Relief agencies like the Red Cross and Red Crescent help people who have been affected by **tsunamis**. They bring food and water and help to find homes for survivors.

The Red Cross delivers packages of food and water to help tsunami survivors.

Stopping Tsunamis?

People cannot stop **tsunamis** from happening. But they can take steps to make them less devastating.

Some seaside villages in Sri Lanka without forests were destroyed by the 2004 tsunami. But villages with **mangrove** forests growing near the water were not. The trees stopped the advance of the tsunami. A village in India with a forest of tall casuarina trees also escaped the destruction.

People can protect existing mangrove forests or plant new forests to help protect them from tsunamis.

People can also learn the warning signs of tsunamis. That way, they will know when to leave an area and go to higher ground.

In Indonesia, this man is planting mangrove trees. When the trees grow they may protect his village from future tsunamis.

THE MARINE SOCIETY AND SEA CADETS
THOMAS GRAY MEMORIAL TRUST

AWARD OF MERIT

Tilly Smith

Tilly Smith

Tilly Smith received an award for saving lives.

Tilly's warning

In 2004 a 10-year-old British girl named Tilly Smith vacationed with her family at a resort in Thailand. She had studied tsunamis in school. When the ocean pulled back, Tilly knew a killer wave was coming. She and her father warned hotel workers. Everyone at the resort left the beach just before the tsunami crashed down. Tilly's education and quick thinking saved many lives.

Saving Lives

There is no way to stop **tsunamis** once an **earthquake** has set off these giant waves. But warning centers can identify possible tsunamis and alert people to the danger. Then people can survive by staying out of the water and quickly leaving dangerous areas.

This map shows how far the 2004 tsunami reached in the hours after the earthquake.

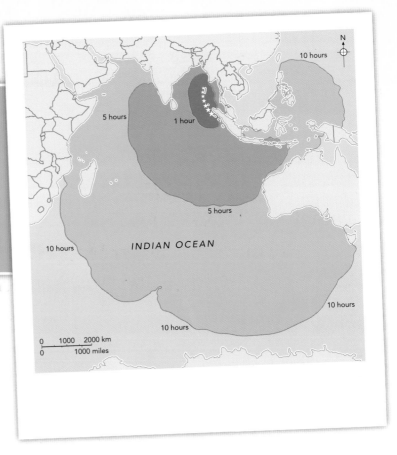

Around the world, scientists collect information about undersea earthquakes and tsunamis. This helps them warn people before the giant waves strike.

In the United States, the **DART**® **system** consists of special **buoys** (floating objects attached to the ocean floor). Machines placed on the ocean floor record if a tsunami is passing by. They send this information to the buoys. The information is then immediately sent to various warning centers, like the Pacific Tsunami Warning Center in Hawaii and the West Coast/Alaska Tsunami Warning Center.

Special buoys can sense where tsunamis are headed.

Do animals know?

Animals may sense when tsunamis are coming. Before the 2004 tsunami in Thailand, a herd of elephants suddenly ran to higher ground in the hills. Before giant waves hit southern India, a herd of wild antelope ran from the coast to higher forests.

Glossary

aftershock smaller earthquake that follows a main earthquake

bacteria microscopic (very tiny) living things

buoy floating object that is attached to the ocean floor

continental plate tectonic plate that lies under the continents

core Earth's center

crust top layer of Earth

DART ® system system that is used to find out when underwater earthquakes occur, so that scientists can predict when tsunamis might occur

earthquake strong shaking of the top of Earth caused by forces underneath Earth

fault very big crack in Earth's crust

magma hot, melted rock that comes from deep inside Earth

malaria deadly disease spread by infected mosquitoes

mangrove tree that grows in tropical climates. Mangroves have very large roots.

mantle layer of Earth that sits below the crust and above the core

oceanic plate tectonic plate that lies below the oceans

Richter scale numbers that are used to measure the strength of an earthquake

Ring of Fire area surrounding the Pacific Ocean, where hundreds of volcanoes are located. Most of the world's earthquakes occur there.

shock wave shaking that starts at one place and moves out, shaking the ground in all directions

tectonic plate part of Earth's crust that floats over a layer of Earth called the mantle. Tectonic plates fit together like a big jigsaw puzzle.

tidal wave unusually large wave caused by wind and the tides

tide natural rising and falling of the ocean

tsunami giant wave caused by underwater earthquakes, landslides, and volcanoes

volcano mountain with an opening where lava, gas, and rocks can shoot out

Find Out More

Books to read

Do you still have questions about **earthquakes** and **tsunamis**? There is much more to learn about these fascinating topics. You can find out more by picking up some of these books from your local library:

Morrison, Taylor. *Tsunami Warning*. Boston: Houghton Mifflin Company, 2007.

Spilsbury, Louise, and Richard Spilsbury. *Sweeping Tsunamis (Awesome Forces of Nature)*. Chicago: Heinemann Library, 2005.

Townsend, John. *The Asian Tsunami 2004 (When Disaster Strikes)*. Chicago: Raintree, 2007.

Websites to explore

Learn cool facts about earthquakes through animations, puzzles, and more at this government website:
http://earthquake.usgs.gov/learning/kids

Check out this government site to find out how to protect yourself, your family, and your pets during a tsunami emergency:
www.fema.gov/kids/tsunami.htm

Take a Tsunami Trivia Quiz, look at tsunami signs from around the world, and more at this Pacific Tsunami Museum site:
www.tsunami.org

Index